BLUE CHEVIES

Jim Klein

Publisher: Lulu.com

Editor: Mark Fogarty

Editorial Advisor: Melanie Klein

Designer: Tony Fradkin

ISBN: 978-0-557-00240-5

Distributed by:

WHITE CHICKENS PRESS

PO Box 1691

Rutherford, NJ 07070

Contents

"It's just steel, it will eventually give up."
—Gromer Wilkie

Acknowledgements

Thanks to the editors of the following journals where these poems (some with different titles) first appeared: *Dirty Napkin*: "Blue Chevies." / *Fatlip*: "I Didn't Know if I Was Afoot or on Horseback." / *Gandhabba*: "Vastly in the Present." / *Journal of New Jersey Poets*: "Greenhorns," "You Two." / *Mudfish*: "The Way Some People Dress Blind People," "Tossing Firewood," "Lake Campbell." / *Onthebus*: "Cleaning Pheasants." / *Rt. 80*: "For Harry Walsh." / *The Rutherford Red Wheelbarrow*: "The Apple," "Darwin's Burden," The Furring Strip and the Pear," "The Goat," "Versus," "Salmon, Not Whales." / *The Wormwood Review*: "Colonel Sanders Fried Chicken," "Gromer Wilkie."

Back cover photo: Rob Quatrone.

Shining Through the Mends: Jim Klein's Poetic Economies

After my sister died, I went to Alaska to be at the dedication of a house built only by women in her honor. The woman in charge of the build, Arlene Patton (inevitably called the General), said that her father had told her there were three things you had to do to claim a successful life: raise a family, read the Bible from beginning to end, and build a house with your own hands. The General had now done all three.

I'm reminded of this by Jim Klein's indelible book of poetry, *Blue Chevies*, because it opens and closes with poems concerned, among other things, with life lists like hers. In its opening poem, "Urned," the poet comes across a few of his father's things on a dresser, "minutia of male economy" like a half stick of gum, a couple of Sen Sen, bits of tinfoil. And immediately he's set out a key theme of *Blue Chevies*: its economically told arc of the male cycle from father-to-son and boy-to-man-to-father-himself, in poems pushed out onto the highway with all the efficiency of a pit stop by an Indy crew.

Remembering his father's death and life in this first poem, Jim returns to his native Dakotas, a place where nostalgia and alienation mix as (un)easily as oil and water, a place that summons up matter-of-fact images like his father killing a chicken. Or images that balance memories of a disastrous encounter with canned whipped cream, waffles and applesauce with his father's graceful turn at a church supper, balancing a loaded plate through a series of contortions without dropping any of the food.

Taking us quickly through his father's life and decline (the pun is to honor the triple pun in the title of this poem, the father being named Ernst), Klein then quotes from his father's list of things for a man to accomplish to earn a good life: "to ride a horse/to shoot a rifle/to site a building." Jim's poem of life and death and male legacy is then unsentimental enough to repeat his father's remark that one of those buildings was sited off-kilter.

"Urned" ends, though, in a typical and brilliant turn, after the laconic recitals of his father's existence and the jokey references to his funeral urn, with an economical touch of feeling and father-honoring struck with just one swift touch of the poet's palette: the seemingly offhand "something about roses." Appropriate for a funeral!

Many of the themes in "Urned" are mirrored in the wonderful poems that end *Blue Chevies*. In "Afoot or On Horseback," Jim, like his father, reflects on what he wants his own tombstone to say. And in "The Goat," this time it's Jim who is a grown man helping to kill a goat for a wedding feast, discharging a tradition for the brother-in-law and father of the bride in his wife's native Trinidad. This last poem is laid out in the same eight economical stanzas as "Urned" is, and Jim's cutting up goat earns him an accolade at the Second Sunday supper not unlike his father's artful choreography must have inspired at the church supper: Jim is a man of "plenty-plenty." And this acknowledgement of manhood inspires him to reflect on his own understated life list, which is to be born and to live every day.

In the middle of the book, and the arc, is the title sequence. "Blue Chevies" is a serious/funny deconstruction of the romantic poem tradition. No Shakespeare and Dark Lady nor Dante and Beatrice here: Jim's beloved is wooed in a parking lot full of old cars behind a bar and ends up passed out on the back seat of one. She also likes to piss outdoors, "with moonbeams bouncing/ off her ass." The poet's declaration of love's transforming effect extends only so far as the seemingly offhand "Until I loved you,/ I never knew/ there were so many/ blue Chevies."

But wait a minute. To the first sight this is anti-romantic diffidence personified. But look at the internal rhyme of you-knew-blue. And the ending near-rhyme of "many" and "Chevies." This is craftily not so far from the moon-June-spoon of besotted romantic lyricists. And think about those blue Chevies a little more. To my mind the image conjured is a block-long blue 1960 convertible Cadillac a neighbor of my parents owned, one of the most romantic cars ever engineered in Detroit. There can be few more romantic bursts than the transformative power of love that allows you to see you live in a universe of big, blooming blue cars. Bravo!

Mixed in between these three defining poems we have a bunch of poems that trace Jim's journey from his Midwest upbringing and young manhood to his present life in New Jersey, poems presented in short clear narrative clips that often end in moments as stunning as the closing couplets of sonnets. (In fact, if I didn't know better, I'd say Klein writes busted up anti-sonnets, deliberately dynamiting the elaborate form but keeping the Mike Tyson KO punch at the end.) Take "Tossing Firewood," for instance. It starts in low gear with the funny observation that cars look like people or they wouldn't sell. Then it progresses to the aerodynamic differences in the firewood logs the poet is tossing on a pile. Then comes the knockout punch: "Grace doesn't come from above./ It shines through the mends." *Blue Chevies* contains many such Tyson bout-enders. Here's another one, from "Darwin's Burden:" "Even the angels are uncertain/if they are walking among the living/or the dead."

There are also great poems about Midwestern types like the unforgettable junkyard dealer Gromer Wilkie, with his immortal rust stains, and his artist-like ability to lay a straight bead of welds. Gromer is a kind of presiding saint in the world of this book, and it's not too hard to imagine him cutting a blue Chevy in half for the sheer joy of welding it together again.

Gromer's life wisdom is given glancingly in an e-mail Klein later received (it also serves as the book's epigraph): "It's just steel, it will eventually give up." This can apply to many non-welding situations as well!

Later poems abound in images from Klein's not-quite-bucolic New Jersey, where he has worked as a teacher at several colleges. Klein lives currently in Rutherford, NJ, the hometown of William Carlos Williams, the most influential poet in American history. Like Williams, he is a close observer of events in nature. Also like Williams, he keeps his language simple and direct. Klein is not as bare-bones as Williams was in his groundbreaking poetic examinations of smalltown minutia, like plums in the fridge or the famous red wheelbarrow. That ground has been broken. Klein follows after Williams, along the arc he described, but doesn't need to directly imitate the master.

Klein does tend to follow Williams' lead in sticking to the real, and eschewing the abstract. He does take up philosophical topics every so often, but usually prefers to take a seat and wait until the urge passes. He does think some about the burden of living in a post-Darwin world with no metaphysical certainties, but he'd much rather describe the polluted river water of the Passaic River. "The bark of any tree/is better than causality," he concludes in another sprung sonnet couplet.

Jim Klein is a top-rank American poet. He's published more than 100 poems in the *Beloit Poetry Journal*, the *Berkeley Review*, all the usual places. He's reached the final rounds in the last couple of years of the Anthony Hecht and Sawtooth Poetry Prizes, and has had a special section in *Wormwood Review*. He's an active part of the Rutherford poetry revival, as a member of the WCW Poetry Collective and leader of the Red Wheelbarrow Poets there. He has started two literary journals in Rutherford, the unruly *Lunch* and the smart, energetic *Rutherford Red Wheelbarrow Poets Anthology*. But he's never published a book.

That may seem puzzling, but gradually you can see why when you read the sly, spare, graceful poems that make up *Blue Chevies*. You see the beautiful economy with which he has sketched out a poetry concerned with the hard-earned wisdom of many years of clear-eyed observation. Klein has worked on these poems for years, polishing off the rough edges, considering where each line should break, where each stanza should start, which poem should follow which poem. The poems of *Blue Chevies* have been worked on until they shine through each of the mends he has made in them.

That's why the publication of this artfully constructed and thoughtfully considered book is such an occasion, and a cause for celebration. I'm glad to have had a hand in editing and publishing it. Read it under the trees while you watch the cars passing by, and give thanks for being alive and for living every day.

MARK FOGARTY

Blue Chevies

Urned

1

A stick of Dentyne
twisted in half,
Sen-Sen bounced out
of the little red box
on the dresser: minutia
of male economy.
Not a collection, string balls
or matchstick furniture,
but real tiny effects
(other than writing
or a strict toting up),
bits of tinfoil, a found
object in a jacket pocket
whereby a monster tomorrow
might be counterweighted,
Destiny as ripping
and saving motions
with scrap paper,
taming paint out
of a can with a stick,
off the lip .

2

Magical against wood,
it took him miss miss miss
blam on chicken neck.
Blood flecks on his sleeve
so beautiful I thought
of French cuffs.
I've just remembered
cleaning pheasants:
little nooses hanging
in the basement,
blood drops dropping,
newspapers spread out
like my excitement,
slicking the breasts clean
of bird turf,
the raw breasts swinging,
the story of each crop
he showed me
with his thick thumb.

3

If that tree's gone
that's not my boyhood home.
Denuded, no way
to get to the roof,
no leafy mediator,
no crow's-nest to
wait in for my cousins
to come and go fishing,
to come and do
nothing less than fill in
our incompletenesses:
wheel turning along the curb,
yelling *Hello!* from the eaves
Hello! from the tree: gone
fish: gone   us: gone
all all all gone

4

We had applesauce
on our waffles once,
with canned whipped cream,
just invented.
What's funny is
waffles and applesauce
are on the ceiling!
And my father's face!
We're all laughing
and crying,
my father's swearing
in German
and spraying
and waffles and applesauce
are exploding
all over the place.

5

At church suppers, my father piled up a plate
with two slabs of meat loaf, scalloped potatoes,
orange jello, black olives, one or two deviled eggs,
and a big yawn of chocolate cake and atop
the fingers of his right hand slowly back
in past his hip rotating it back until it
was behind him going dangerously out up
over beyond his shoulder still somehow
back down flat (grin) then up the other
way and back down around again.

6

Not even trying to march the kazoo band
has straggled into the brain
of this locale, putting all business
to a halt and installing Chef Lester
in a pickup with a bunch of kids
banging on pots and pans
and all you goddamn want is to live
to see one more crummy Fourth of July
parade through Ocean Park again.
Through all that rain, this must look
just staged enough to be whatever
reality you still figure to run into
with your shaved head and beret.

7

Yes, I see how
that wouldn't work, he says.

And the job
is exactly as bad

as leaning into
his back at an angle.

And he takes awhile
at the sink.

8

Room With a View

When I shall have done
with these elements
place my
urn
at the foot
of a pitch pine
whose grubby branches
on the coldest winter
night
embrace
the north wind
and all the
stars.
EK 11-30-77

A car pulls into a driveway deep in shadow
and focus falls on a tipped beach chair
by the rock garden: a wedge of old man
powerless to get back in.
He's right. Lots of this is funny.

To eschew a gravestone,
to be emptied into an urn instead;
then to be planted between
twin scrub pine
beneath a brass plaque
inscribed with his own poem:
he would have said he had *urned* it.

To ride a horse,
to shoot a rifle,
to site a building.

Something to live by.
The garage came out a bit high.

On his hands and knees,
he dug out four feet of sand
at the south end.

For what?
He told me, but I forgot.
Something about roses.

Gromer Wilkie

His junkyard is an oxide jungle.
Even inside his abundance takes root.
Rusty chains creep up
from the ferrous underfoot
to brown blossoms
rank on his fat pillars.
Tools hang dead ripe.

Men squat watching Gromer.
He's the only one in town
to weld on Sundays
or to have the nickel rods
to braze a manifold.
Once he cut a truck in half
and welded it back.

Gromer knows how
to make his little bit,
and how to help them
make their little bit too.
He lays a pretty good bead.

Schiff Estates

August afternoon rings
in our ears and warps
this tiny trailer space
while Mike Schiff
drives down iron
to tidy up
the drainage ditch.
His presence requires
a deeper time,
and we are cilia in a lung,
wildflowers swaying
on the windy plains,
and Mike Schiff
stops driving iron
and the ditch runs
wild beneath us.

You Two

All right, you two.
I'm looking through your house
for evidence of the real *you two*.
Where is one of those lousy white bread
and Velveeta sandwiches?
With words I dissect the marriage
you took ten years to stretch out prone dead
on the slab your house was built on.
Surely, your own words seek replies.
But not my replies. Not replies mentioning
scratches on my forearms or the throwing
of a bag of groceries against the wall.
Surely, you two must still agree,
at least, about me.

Changing into Swimming Suits in the Car

Behind us is everything to win or lose drunkenly
fumbling through its own transformations.
But there are times not to look back,
even when a rationale for irregular behavior
is so strongly around it may already
have reached the point of legitimacy.

After all, there is a harder counterpart
of what you think you are on the seat beside you,
and though he may profit equally, he is,
despite past actions, another stranger,
and being involved at present in the quick
motions of his own vulnerability,
he is even more so. Or not.

The cubical seatings of advanced societies
are full of oaken meanings.

Yet there are times for letting the girls drive,
as though there were no preferred direction at all.

In fact, driving around aimlessly
is almost always best.

Franklin, Indiana

There lives within my bones
a quality of loss:
the inability of towns
to comport themselves sensibly
without a courthouse square
radiating as Franklin, Indiana does.
I feel a dearth of anchors
like Shine Weddel and Bear Soup,
vice lords in two pool halls
fixed on the square.
Saturday nights at Shine's,
farm hands pissed
in a blackened sink
and tithed ten times to evil.
I've lived other places,
but life loses its factual stickum
without a courthouse square.

For Harry Walsh

While he was up to his elbows in poems,
clattering the poems together and banging
the poetry on the cans of Budweiser
with milky loops around their middles,
I set my daughter to bringing apples
from the front yard, two each trip,
a task she began with the enthusiasm
of those who have never had to work,
and finding myself left alone,
I stretched out on the fallen leaves,
rolled into the fallen autumn
and dreamt of a giant circle
up into the poem tree.

The Eames Chair

For a moment I was almost reminded
of a Danish modern chair.
Not that Danish modern
is the last word.
The Eames chair is.
His idea was that the armpit
is a design problem
God hasn’t solved yet.
But we were almost a chair,
so there’s still, don’t you think, hope?

Different Trees

These things hit you while you're zipping up.
The further you go, the lonesomer, of course.
You'll never be without your father,
that goes without saying,
but your father's not along.
Yours is never really his gesture.
You don't know why your shoulders roll so,
maybe another kid on the playground.
But you're coming along.
It's a different world.
Different cooking,
different doors and degrees.
Different trees.

The Way Some People Dress Blind People

Those who paint stone walls and the trunks of trees;
aluminum siding stamped with wood grain.
There's a house in Hawthorne with an aqua car,
aqua-painted stones along the driveway.
Water stones. Water car.
The blind singer at the piano
singing his own pain
dressed in other people's clothes.

We're a bubble of taste and hilarity anyway,
rolling through New Jersey.
Wonderfully terrible, the lopsided
welded shelving uprights, painted red,
a small octagon inside another shape,
still very modest in size.

But there are compensations:
Lucy, I do love you still
painted on the side of the Pathmark.
Real love poetry
left unhindered for months.

Good bye, little person.
I love you.

Keep on,
against tremendous odds.

Tossing Firewood

We just put up a small building
designed by an Indian architect.
It has no heating.
Cars look like people
or they wouldn't sell.
Another theory holds that cars,
which used to look like trains,
presently resemble
nothing so much as TV sets.
Tossing firewood, I notice
every log has its own aerodynamics.
I like you. I think you're smart.
I trust your alcoholism and fishing.
Grace doesn't look down.
It shines through the mends.

Bock Beer

Wide over your face.
I have no idea what it means either,
but I mean it,
and I want to write a poem
that begins *wide,*
wide over your face.

Bock beer.
I also like bock beer.
You don't like bock beer,
you like green bottles,
but I want to sit, my back to you,
drink bock beer and write
hard between us.

Rye. Wide over your rye.
$30 worth, blue grass and nitrogen.
An old man told me lime sweetens the soil,
one of the most encouraging things
I've heard in a long time.

Just now in the back yard,
I discovered some of the old time
sowing motions, almost like golf.
I should tell you these things.
Lime sweetens the soil.
Every old man has a bag.

Vastly in the Present

Here's the thing; no need to get inside.
The randy surface of things is thing enough.
Just watch the bubbles slide downstream.
If you see a beautiful woman,
do you want to talk to her?
Let me tell you, friend, what is
is two years old, permanently.
Long speeches in French
in the middle of the night
(and nobody speaks French).
The bark of any tree
is better than causality.

Heraldry

Early some cold March morning,
I'll take a hatchet and hit
the bark off a spindly tree.
I'll gather those gleanings
and cover your thighs and eyes,
your arms and hair,
until you roll under those chips
like pushed water in a bog,
wet with medals.

Heavy-Duty Sensibility

A flower was her face,
a round vowel,
a collision of two or three
held notes, nothing
to be gathered and rolled.
But there's more in any second
storming by like boxcars,
even if you're not counting
or waiting for open doors
on both sides,
just that much rattling,
banging, barn-colored machinery.
How do you compare
going down the road
to wailing freight trains,
crashing bashing engines
of fate and fortune,
the widely-sought-after
crushing opponent,
or a teenage girl who runs faster
that you race anyway,
securely within something
greater than you can spit
in the face of or hold
lovingly in your arms
outside of all harm.

Blue Chevies

1

The parking lot behind George and Eddie's
pushes back in a jagged shape.
We have one working car engine,
one heater, six Rheingolds,
a joint of "good Colombian,"
and a country music station.
Two empty cars are frozen in with us.
We keep expecting their owners,
who never come. We kiss, often
glancing out at the snowdrift
piling up by the side door,
red from the Schaefer sign.

2

Used to spend free afternoons
speeding on two-lane Indiana highways.
Continued existence due to the savvy
and foresight of oncoming motorists.

Easterners in the Midwest complain
they are surrounded by cornfields.
The East, to me, was the reverse:
no way to get out of town.
Just west on Rt. 3 felt like release.

Totowa
a case of beer
and Thou!

Red neon sign (out of repair)
STRAT   MO

tv $12, no tv $11
no tv

3

Until I loved you,
I never knew
there were so many
blue Chevies.

4

An early spring morning,
the sky's a silver coin,
and we haven't been to bed,
if that is the truth, and maybe it is,
that would be something.
But the truth, as I understand it,
is probably doomed.
Right now, the truth is passed out
in the back seat of her car.
Besides, I'm sick of the truth.
The truth is very free with herself.
The truth is beautiful
and stays beautiful through a lot of abuse.
The truth is heavy to carry too.
By herself, the truth can't take care of the truth.
In fact, the truth's a real punishment to be around.
But if the truth's not involved, I don't care.

5

George called yesterday
to say he had some bad news.
For once George didn't exaggerate.
I sat down to eat again.
In the driveway, my landlord
was spray painting a fender
in a motion like the Almighty
wiping you out.

6

She gave me her breast
in a bar
out the neck
of a red sweater.

She knew every cop
and bartender.
She ran everywhere
she went.

She loved pissing
out of doors,
bouncing moonbeams
off her ass.

Everyone
should be understood,
at least once.

George and Eddie's

He just squeezes his thumb over
to make a bridge,
and he puts his other thumb
on top of the cue, steering,
which is wrong.

Eddie's got cataracts.

Your first ball is your pocket:
you have to make the 8-ball there.

Play to win,
or don't play at all, young fellow!
I've got all the time in the world
to play pool with nice people.

Good break!
You've got the little ones
and the juke box.

Big Foot

"Big Foot" isn't bad
as nicknames go.
And his poem
is a pretty good brief
for kicking some bastard in,
if not this one,
to wit: he's the one
being kicked by a world
wearing his boots.

Maybe he's only toeing
his own cuckolder,
already held down
and having the piss
pounded out of him
by her husband.
Anyway, he goes over
and starts kicking.

Herringbone

In a long afternoon, no one shows off.
Contributions are as complementary
as herringbone.
The hum is rare music.
But the bolt of this fabric has been lost.
Lapping conversation is jostled
like a dirty birdbath.
Company departs with a broken heart,
if it has one, and the vivid
display of character fritters away
into picking up the house.
The bones of contention
are rolled into the trash.
The people stay.

Colonel Sanders Fried Chicken

Her husband, she's so embarrassed she has to break in
and tell him his thinking is so full of stereotypes,
not all black people believe in voodoo, she says,
and he says children shouldn't be spanked,
they should have their fingers cut off
and their parents should order
Colonel Sanders Fried Chicken
and give them the terrible time of trying
to eat fried chicken with no fingers,
turning cupped hands toward her
to demonstrate the difficulty
of fingerless fried chicken eating.

On the Loveliness of Our Intimate Repose

Prettily quartered by the imaginary
line of eyelashes crossing
your nose above sleep-pursed lips
your child-like face lies anuzzle
on a red feather cushion.
Your fingers droop to piano keys.
Beyond orange-round knees
veeing down to the vein-blue ankle
bent over your poor callused little toe,
a woman's magazine lies open
on your blind breasts
while, to tick tock, bird chirp,
and refrigerator whirr,
I sit savoring Nabokov's
itches and tickles
until I am moved to reach
for a yellow legal pad,
partly torn and dried-paste stiff,
crosshatched *We* and *They*,
cradling the eggs of round numbers,
to begin with the bleeding end
of a red felt tip pen
these notes on the loveliness
of our intimate repose.

Alan

I sat here all summer
under your books
like *i* bent to *e*
dreaming of
snapping to
with such a jolt
as to toss my dot
five lines up into
the paragraph
your bookshelves
make and glanced
to the left margin
where a cardinal
looped red poems
on the trellis
and tacked them
down with his
orange nose.

Greenhorns

Even sleeping past noon is no defense
against drunken arguments
continuous through my sleep,
but lighting up
and looking out at the day,
sunlight on snow
which was a bitch last night,
the landlord's young wife
is shoveling down the sidewalk
with him sauntering after her
opening an envelope.
It really must be good news
because at the curb he shows her,
and her face glows
against the fresh snow.

Making Love with Real Bad Head Colds

We're enough after all these years,
we can make love
with real bad head colds:
we kiss in a way
we can still breathe.
We go at it panting
and rattling away.
We don't break up
no matter how we sound.

Little Moon

Little moon, you're a triangle,
almost, in the dusk tonight,
and I can almost see
what I only first saw
when I looked through
my neighbor's binoculars,
that your blurred edge curves
toward me. Now I can *see* it
with a naked eye, and I wonder
that the ancients, not knowing
what to look for, couldn't.

I envy the man I should know,
could probably guess,
who discovered the secret
of your chimerical light.
You were a keyhole
through which he saw,
not a monster, but a bit
of a highly intriguing game,
which, he must have seen,
had been going on a long time,
and, of which, contrary
to experience, he was a part.

You gave him a heart-beating
moment, little star,
like in a palace somewhere
when some loafers,

playing with ranks and files,
buttons and odd medals,
invented the knight
and began seeing around corners
and hopping over each other.

Shop-Rite

A 48-year-old gourmet
who boasts of being friends
with Tony Provenzano
drops dead one morning
walking his puppy
and Shop-Rite never stops,
keeps rite on ticking.
William Carlos Williams' son
grows up to be a baby doctor.
One winter afternoon, slightly drunk,
I carried my daughter into
the wrong door at 9 Ridge Road
and Flossie was asleep
on the couch with the soaps on,
her hair tinted blue that day.

Diagramming Ideas

Diagramming ideas,
which is my job in a way,
at times, to entertain students,
isn't really the chalky shell game it seems,
but more like making an incision
in an area not properly tied off
because before I can show them,
the argument has pumped itself
full of blood, and overflowed itself,
and saved itself in red confusion.

Patty's House

First time I expected a fist fight;
she wore a long dress.
She made me a wet martini in a chilled glass.
I agreed to a tossed salad.
She sliced cheese into a long thin bits.
Her words were as clean as celery snapping.
Upstairs, there was a refrigerator
full of Rheingold, a stereo,
and Elvis Presley records.
She said if she ever got married
she'd cheat with me for 100 years.

Max

If poetry is the manipulation
of levels of abstraction,
and I believe it is,
why can't the poet
work all the time
like the painter does?
        Max says,
"Not tongue and groove,
or mortar and pestle.
You have to remember
the Cavalier poets,
Sir Walter Raleigh.
The poet writes his poem
between the saddle
and the ground."

Dark Glasses on a Serious Nose

So love is overwhelmingly aesthetic,
and largely visual at that,
a feigned levity,
superior gesturing,
dark glasses lowered
on a serious nose.
Consider the Beloved,
a rotary rose garden,
the firmer curves
of artful victories
maybe, or maybe not,
diverting traffic
on a right hand bias,
I honestly don't know.
What we do know
is that ants walk around
putting down random
goo dots, and only
when two goos get close
do they start thinking
arches and order
lifts its awful head.

Sand Worms

First thing on board,
Kenny hooked a dollar bill
and his can of sardines
onto a spreader he had just bought
and jerked them up and down
over the water until they fell in
to the amusement of the old black men
on another party boat.
We left the dock.
When it was discovered
we had spent $8 on sand worms
when clams and fiddler crabs were free,
the question became what to do
with the sand worms?
We put them in the coffee,
but we soon saw
we'd have to eat
the sand worms too.

Instead, for Ray

Not for the parachutist who lands
on an X atop a flying balloon,
not for the maker
of an arm prosthesis,
not for Vic Fahri
teaching investments.
Instead, for Ray, this time
in the guise of a man trying
to figure something out,
even when it's something
as trivial as who Patty
will sleep with tonight.
The inability to find out
what you have no business
knowing is so human.
And Ray's an honest man.
He looks across the bar
with the fixed, squint
eye of a carpenter.

Vincent

Perfect is occasionally rigged brilliantly by the lucky few
who have sneaked beyond the bounds.
But why must everything be nailed down?
It comes at us unglued, in the barber's chair.
The neighbor's wife died six months ago.
The barber himself was an orphan at nine,
saw his father twice a year, at the orphanage,
didn't want to, describes himself
as growing up a stranger, a little soldier,
talking quietly in his crowded shop.

The Dorf

Three tough old men sit
at the midpoints
of a three-sided bar.
A cue drops; a girl laughs.
Just because it's done so casually,
someone's engaged in a vital game of chess.
Why anyone should believe anyone else
is, or is not, why a hand or a life
should be proffered in healthy expectation,
why the favorites should win
and the curve of Freitag's triangle
come in is a real puzzler.

Regarded on the sudsy spill,
we're all the same.
This is my room,
and I don't understand it.
In others, those with Oriental rugs,
I do worse.
I can be the shower stall
for your singing only.
Watching someone else get better
is a progress so slow,
so without a *telos*
that sometimes I think
the world's perfect indifference
is better than the best teaching.

The Art of Reading

The impeccably dressed short man
on the cake isn't just not tall.
He's seized his moment
under these pines,
his own stereo lugged here,
Brahms cum pine cones,
to give a little whistle stop.
There's a painting,
"The Art of Reading,"
where the pictorial planes
have been distorted to make space
for the text to balloon into.

Yet the moment goes.
You can't marry a Jew
without breaking a glass.
Life is more like a conductor
with a broken elbow
or a student DJ introducing
a record snatched at random,
a Japanese big band, it turns out,
recorded in 1972, having
musicians with unanimously
unpronounceable names.

Lake Campbell

This row of men at the bar
reminds me of the perch,
numerous as leaves,
holding the slack line
in the sides of their mouths
in the green water of Lake Campbell.
Someone leans over and whispers
he wants to blow his brains out.

Beautiful woman, you're the poem.
Rain on the roof, bass booming below,
and you warm all over me
like blood in the dirty attic bed.

These Beans Are Mine

Blue hills darken;
light rises in parallel lines.
Three men come up,
go away as a monster
with three backs.
Someone new comes up,
comes up again.
Not none of the blowhead ones.
To be loved requires
the steady thinking.
They are measuring by the big tree
where I do not go.
I lie down on the wet bank.
This is good enough for now.

Film Noir

When, in Faulkner, the horse is so wild
he's never seen shucked corn,
and, to him, the kernels look like bugs,
that's about it.

The guard's from Tennessee.
He stands by the door
where there's never
been a guard before.

Your body is less than all the times
I've touched it.

What shall we call the corn?

The corn is bugs.
That would be my way.

The Trace

Running across the bridge
over the Passaic River
I raise my arms in triumph
and run under open palms
like a held-aloft cup
and salute upriver,
wondering what those
in their cars are thinking of,
and, leaving 3 West,
I flywheel downgrade
into the brown grass
on the cloverleaf,
following the trace
torn by yesterday's run.

"Declinism"

My old pilotings are the music
to avoid right now.

Something beyond witty literalism
would be nice;

what the French are calling “declinism”
might be more in order,

fairy dust inventively rendered
while vaguely under the influence

of Handel’s Concerto No. 6,
quantities of green tea,

and these blessedly free Fridays.
It’s not a great world

to grow up in,
but it’s gorgeous,

and it’s never going
to define my life.

Escarole Lettuce

I’ve got all the time in the world
to be intermittently great,
to become outrageous
and patient enough
to bring together bits and pieces
that don’t necessarily mean
anything on their own
but evoke a world
as savory and unrestrained
as a Mediterranean salad.

I was so sure firm bottoms
was what was wanted,
a drink served over cracked ice,
when something like a woman’s
hybrid item of apparel
seems much more fitting,
produce blowing out of the poem
instead of receding into it
like a medicine cabinet,
which isn’t at all to say
that I should eschew obfuscation
and escarole lettuce.

Darwin's Burden

1

We take comfort in believing
that time acts in a certain way.

Too bad we're wrong.

What constitutes a moment in time,
and even space,
is completely subjective.

With each step,
I further fracture Newton's
pristine and uniform conceptions,
concentration camps without fences.

2

We might as well ask what is art?

Is it tormented drifters
and the devil at the crossroads,

the lushness and sensuality of Brazil,

a big step forward toward grittier
and more tumultuous experiences?

A poet's feelings for the half said,
an interest in the old in itself, is OK.

3

No brain event happens the same way twice.
Even memory is always a variant—

a recreation, never a repetition,
more metaphor than logic.

There is no one standing behind the curtain—
Darwin's burden.

Even the angels are uncertain
if they are walking among the living
or the dead.

Serenity Poem

Some mistakes are so big and so dumb
that the only response is silence

a hatred so pure, so solemn,
it feels beautiful, almost holy.

Noon

Zorida in her
frilly dress

in her own
lawn towards

a wavering butterfly
above the pink

impatiens with
her careful in

the air quick
brown hand.

Beethoven

Art is getting your butt
kicked I can't
get Williams out of
my mind, for example.
Ever Oedipal, Pal.
Who cares about your
whining the thing is
to get in there
and pitch.
Bring it sideways
out of your ass
since you're
not Mozart.
Fight for every
note. It's just
as lovely
as fighting
them off.

The Furring Strip and the Pear

I am the furring strip angled longingly
in the arm of the pear tree

awaiting the little black girl and her dad
on their way home from Union School

for their use to joust you down, lone pear,
aloft for months like a Tiffany *objet*.

Other years, pears aplenty
like suds on the Passaic River,

but this year squirrels
like flame throwers.

Unreasonable! Unseasonable!
No berries on the dogwood either!

Oh pear, how have you kept yourself so chaste
where no squirrel can reach you?

Of everyone, only the little girl saw you,
and, by her father's strong brown arm

and my blunt end, she shall have you!

The Structure of Cubism Emerging

In this Woolworth's photo booth,
1963, we might almost
be taken for siblings.
No clenched power shows
in these fading likenesses
with great smiles in this tiny picture
beside our daughter's computer,
just youth's soft and edgeless patches,
but I was a leaper before a looker
and you were all stoic monumentality.
Always beautiful, but heavy in hand,
you were not the love of my life,
though, in ways, she has been mine.

Boys Chorus

All these years waiting
for NYC to seek me
among the Rutherfordians.

Yet even Cezanne
wasn't too proud
to take lessons from Pissaro.

At some point, Charlie Parker
had to stop playing
the same song in a different key
in his mother's living room
in Kansas City.

After a year,
Honi Coles had to
come out of the house
and tap.

(No use fumbling around
for humble examples.)

Boys chorus, 7:30 a.m.,
Brookings, South Dakota.

We always tried to sing like cowboys

instead of in that clear voice
that would pierce through anything.

The Apple

This apple I am eating is your body,
Mom, I am biting through the red
tensile skin with a few of the old
front teeth you were once so anxious
and solicitous to feel bumping up
through the repaired gums I have
said and yelled many unkind words
through at you, often in retort.
This is your white juicy
of mixed flavor human flesh
sliding around on the tongue
I have suckled you with and
on which you have embroidered
your wisdoms, like *tea stains,*
and *don't waste food,*
and *it's always something*,
the apple going down and down,
but nothing goes to waste, Mom,
it just goes around and around
like we did, and it really goes,
as I know you know.

Versus

After a bath,
Seagrams's 7
in the wrong glass,
candlelight shattered
on the ceiling: *verse*
comes from the Latin
for where the plow turns.

Salmon, Not Whales

Salmon, not whales,
athletes over intellectuals,
peasants against aristocrats,
gold out of dross in the belief
in character above mere talent,
a void to be filled sentence upon sentence,
not by ambition or pride in difference from others
but in the need and freedom of regret:
what man is, history tells.
I was brought to writing by shame.

The Goat

El Dorado Village, Trinidad

1

I don’t want to kill the animal.
I don’t want to kill the goat.
I don’t want to bring the machete
of subject and predicates down
on Bobby’s wedding for his daughter.

By hack saw, cleaver, and knife,
I don’t want to render
the body and spirit of Boyo
into edible bits,
no matter how delicious.

2

I want the goat whole.
There is nothing to prove to the goat
as Shaffina and her sister watch
in black hajibs from the house.

He doesn’t need to be led by a rope
and relieved of his life
in a little spurting fountain,
or trussed up by a hind leg

in the face of his own cage
beneath the flimsy galvanized
in service to what blank red Vatican
he knows not: the poem.

3

Bobby hangs his hat where he can't reach.
Forty lbs. of garlic, 200 of flour for roti,
heart of palm stacked like whale bones,
and, I'm ashamed to say,
boxes of cubed, frozen goat.

But Bobby has to sell his truck
because sugar cane is a weed in Trinidad now.
Before that, his top-shelf restaurant failed.
And, he has a prior: ten years in the slammer
in Barbados for smuggling drugs.

My wife estimates his "marriages" at four.

4

Light rain drums on the roof,
and I watch from the dung-jewelled pen.
Bobby has more charisma
than any man deserves.
He loiters in across his muddy dump,
roped this last time to his goat.
It doesn't take a genius to see
something mythic is happening,
but like the man being ridden
out of town on a rail,
if it wasn't for the honor,

I'd just as soon walk.

5

There was talk that someone knew the short version,
and someone else the long, but the truth is
that no words as words at all were spoken.

Of course, Bobby's just trying to be a good Moslem
(the rest are Pentecostal),
and maybe killing his good friend
will take his mind off his daughter's wedding.

6

Bobby tips the goat like a dining room table,
and the white-haired, white-capped Old Factotum
dispatches voiceless Boyo fairly routinely.

I admit it. I thought of Daniel Pearl.

7

We hoisted the flapping sacrifice
like an engine in a garage.

Cleaving the hide (whitish inside),
drawing and quartering, as they say,

the phosphorescent guts ballooning
onto the white plastic pail.

At Bobby's order, I retrieved the muddy skin

from beneath the swinging goat.

I divided the coat on the side of the pen
and gave it a little pet.

Just then a little black boy showed up
and began an interrogation.

8

In the car on the way home from Second Sunday,
Halima says, “Jim dance chutney,
Jim cut up goat, Jim plenty plenty.”
Stag is a man’s beer. Guinness is good for you.
Be free of yourself. Chant and be happy.
To be born and to live every day is to kill plenty plenty.

I Didn't Know if I Was Afoot or on Horseback

You can put that on my tombstone
with little fear of vagueness or misunderstanding.
So much for so little must seem remarkable.
What offers itself, finally, is a surface
with all of its gradations and erosions.
Appliances fall back.
The body is scoured into touch.
The life becomes a house;
the house, a city.
Hand and knee leave the ground.

About the Author

JIM KLEIN has had more than 100 poems published in literary journals, including *Beloit Poetry Journal, Berkeley Poetry Review, College English, Field, Gandhabba, Onthebus, Poetry Now, Pulpsmith, Unmuzzled Ox*, and *The Wormwood Review*. A previous version of this book was a 2007 finalist in the Anthony Hecht Award competition, Waywiser Press, and in the Sawtooth Poetry Prize, Ahsahta Press. The leader of The Red Wheelbarrow Poets in Rutherford, NJ, he has started two literary journals there: *Lunch* and *The Rutherford Red Wheelbarrow*.

Appendix — Why Gromer Wilkie Eschewed Gasket Sealer: A Letter from M.D. Kelly

Re: Gromer Wilkie
February 16, 2008 11:05:08 AM EST
"Jim Klein" (jim.klein01@comcast.net)

Greetings from Medina, Ohio.

By way of a one in a million chance, I happened to learn of your poem "Gromer Wilkie" and felt compelled to contact you to learn of your connection to Gromer.

I graduated from the U of I in 1973 and personally benefited from Gromer's talent and expertise on several occasions. He proved invaluable to me in connection with maintaining a 1966 Mustang I stole for $100.00, as well as a project I undertook to change engines in a 1967 Chevy pickup.

Of course that was quite some time ago, but I have continued to engage in limited vehicle maintenance & repair, and over the years I have shared stories about Gromer with friends, relatives, and most of all, my children. I grew up in Charleston, Illinois (south of Champaign). It was a relatively small, rural-flavored community and was blessed with several memorable characters that I still fondly recall,

None, however, were more impressive or had a greater influence on me than Gromer. At that time he lived at the rear of a metal Quonset style building next to his shop, which was an old post & beam barn.

My memories of Gromer are varied, but I recall he eschewed use of gasket sealer, arguing that if the fit was so poor as to require sealer, then it wasn't worth assembling.

I never saw him use a timing light for ignition timing, rather he would have a helper just bump the engine with the starter and he adjusted the distributor by listening to how the engine would recoil.

Nearly the entire floor of his shop was an elevated pad of scrap, old parts, and tools that gradually increased in height by continual accumulation. I remember concluding that he must have had multiple duplicate wrenches, because when he would work on something, it seemed he would just reach down into the pad of debris and obtain the correct tool and simply drop it when he was done.

Occasionally, if he couldn't immediately find the correct tool within arm's reach, he would launch into a rant about his customers being no good thieves.

I can still picture how, over time, welding hose had become irretrievably buried and woven all through the debris that accumulated on the shop floor. In the case his hose would not reach a location, rather than even attempt to untangle the mess, he would simply add another length and continue on, with the new length eventually becoming covered and suffering the same fate.

It was impossible to even guess how many feet the welding gases had to travel from the tank to reach the torch.

When experiencing extreme difficulty and frustration with a mechanical assembly, I still often recall the most lasting quote from Gromer, "It's just steel, it will eventually give up."

After moving away from Champaign, I lost contact with Gromer, but years later, on a trip back home, I took my family past his old shop to see if he was still around. My understanding was that his shop had burned down some years back and the city would not allow him to rebuild. I never heard anything more of Gromer beyond that, until I discovered your poem. What a surprise that was.

Afterword —On an InKleined Plane

My dad taught me most of what I know about poetry. He would write poems around me, leave poems around me. He would leave me around poems, or in the care of poem-writing friends and poem-writing college students. When my chin was about level with its top, he would let me walk with him and other poets around a big table edged with stacks of poems, gathering one page from each stack in the right order, and then let me staple the sheaf from each pass. He'd go to class and say to me, write a poem while I'm gone. He'd look at a poem I'd written and say to me, what kind of a goddamn poem is that?

When I got to be fifteen or sixteen, he would sit me down at the table with his manuscript. He would hand me a pencil, demanding to know what should be better or different, which poems should be taken out, what order was best.

I looked at those poems with awe. They were about his life. They were about being a kid, being a man, having a father. Some were about women (my mother) (others I didn't know, or did). They were about sex, fights, going crazy. Being put in jail, put in the hospital. What could I say about them? I sat there. Miles Davis and Coltrane played *Kind of Blue*; my father made strange stews in the kitchen behind me. I set my elbows on the table and read slowly, making my marks by dim instinct, and then spread the poems out all over the floor and picked them up, one hunch at a time, in a new order.

Then we would go through the manuscript together, him fighting me on almost every suggestion. I learned from his reasons for resisting each change, and I learned from trying to articulate why I believed my change to be crucial. We would do battle over a line break, a word, a comma. This is how I learned what matters to me in a poem.

We still do this. This is how we are together in the world. And I have seen those same poems change form, time beyond measure, for over twenty years.

I saw the lines get shorter; I saw them get longer. Whole sections of poems would get cut, grow back in different form, be shed anew. I saw the stack of old versions on his desk rise to a height of over two feet, lean dangerously, get thrown out, and rise again. (This was years before the computer.) I moved far away, but then manuscripts would arrive by mail. Sometimes I was into it; sometimes I was bored and didn't care; sometimes I was angry and didn't care. Most of the time I wouldn't want to read them, these packed binders. But when I did, I would always be pulled in.

They were always the same poems, plus occasional new growth. They were the same poems, but sometimes a given one among them would be wooden and waterlogged, and other times it would be somehow vibrating, accelerating, lifting off the page. What made the same poem, even with exactly the same words, so different? The smallest change in line ending, a stanza break, the push and pull of the poems placed before and after it. When one of his poems worked, it was thrilling. When one didn't, everything in me wanted it made right. How does it want to be? Where's a pencil?

I've been living back within range for five years now, reading those poems, and new ones, more frequently and more carefully. I returned in time, I think, to witness most of what I perceive as a steady upswing in Jim Klein's powers. Something's been getting into the soil. (I think of the last lines of Williams's "Spring and All.") Early on in my acquaintance with his work, I became aware of a sense, rare but sometimes felt, that the words in a poem were pulling toward each other as I read them, winding image and sound tight around me with the force and effortless grace of gravity, and uncoiling finally, with a bang, against blank space at the end, leaving me peering into nothingness, almost able to see. This feeling—that something true and real is present, palpable and on the verge of visible—is what bound me to poetry. More and more often, these days, even with some of the new ones that I don't yet trust, I get that feeling from Jim Klein's poems.

Work makes these poems what they are. The number of hours, the number of versions each poem passes through—these are incalculable. But it's the nature of the work, not the quantity. There is a clarity of purpose to this. His aim is not (at least not anymore) to be original, or to write like someone else, or even (most of the time) to get published. His aim is simple: to get each poem to where it does what that poem wants to do in precisely the way that poem wants to do it. To get each one there, however long it takes, is what he does. His ear is such that the right words are there from the beginning; the problem is to cut out what is extra and let the poem become itself. And when a poem gets to that point, it has to fight to stay there, for it is tested over and over and over. These poems are here because they are even more stubborn than he is.

My father's dedication and steadiness amaze me, but another quality plays a crucial role in his way of working: his constant drive to learn, to get better, to explore and understand the nature of the poem and how it does what it does. This impulse continually pumps new juice into poems that must otherwise collapse from the strain of what he puts them through. At some point ages ago, he undertook to teach himself traditional metrics, and he spent years searching for the "right" meter for his poems. But then he emerged from that dark hole, having developed a more flexible system of feet that works for his own voice and rhythm and that allows nuances of syntax, rhyme, and meaning to play into where the lines end. This has changed many times over the years, and his use of it grows ever more sure-handed. What he taught himself, and what he is always teaching himself, is how to write a Jim Klein poem.

MELANIE KLEIN

www.ingramcontent.com/pod-product-compliance
Ingram Content Group UK Ltd.
Pitfield, Milton Keynes, MK11 3LW, UK
UKHW020238250726
13967UKWH00001B/443

9 780557 002405